Orangutans

Victoria Blakemore

For Dad, with love

Copyright info/picture credits

Table of Contents

What Are Orangutans?

Orangutans are mammals. They are members of the ape family. Unlike monkeys, apes do not have tails.

There are three different kinds of orangutans: the Sumatran orangutan, the Bornean orangutan, and the Tapanuli orangutan.

The word orangutan means
"man of the forest" in the
Malay language.

Size

Different kinds of orangutans are different sizes. The Bornean orangutans are the largest kind.

Orangutans range in height from about four to five feet. They can weigh up to about 220 pounds.

Male orangutans are usually

larger than female orangutans.

Physical Characteristics

Orangutans have shaggy, red fur. Their fur helps to keep them dry in the wet **climate** of the rainforest.

They have long arms and fingers. This helps them to grip vines and swing through the trees.

Their hands and feet are like human hands. They can be used to climb and grab things.

Habitat

Orangutans are found in rainforests where it is warm and rains a lot.

They spend most of their time in the tall trees. This helps to keep them safe from **predators**. It is also where they find their food.

Range

Orangutans are only found in

parts of Southeastern Asia.

They are mainly found on the

islands of Borneo and Sumatra.

Diet

Orangutans are **omnivores**.

They eat both meat and

plants.

Their diet is made up mostly

of fruit. Their favorite fruits

seem to be mangoes, figs,

and lychees. They also eat

insects, leaves, flowers, and

honey.

Orangutans get much of their protein from ants and termites. They have also been known to eat soil for the minerals.

13

Predators

Orangutans do not have many natural predators. They spend most of their time in the trees, so they are usually safe.

If they do come down to the ground, they could be preyed upon by tigers or leopards.

Orangutans cannot defend

themselves against big cats

like tigers and leopards.

Communication

Orangutans are very intelligent. They are able to communicate with sound, gesture, and touch.

They have a special call called the "long call." It can be heard over a mile away and may last as long as a minute. It is used to warn others about nearby danger.

Orangutans have been known to laugh when they are playing. They may also **mimic** behaviors that they see humans do at zoos.

Movement

Orangutans can move very gracefully through the trees, but they are not fast on the ground. Their top speed is believed to be about four miles per hour.

They don't come down to the ground often because they can't escape predators.

Orangutans even sleep in trees.

They build nests out of twigs

and leaves up high in the trees.

Orangutan Life

Orangutans are usually **solitary** animals. They spend much of their time alone.

They may travel or spend time with other orangutans, but it is usually just for a short time. Males can be very **territorial** and do not like other males too close.

Orangutans are **diurnal**. This means that they are most active during the day.

Young Orangutans

Orangutans usually have one baby. Young orangutans hold onto their mother's stomach or ride piggyback as she moves through the forest.

They stay with their mothers for about 8 years, learning to find food, build nests, and stay safe.

Young orangutans are prey for large predators. They spend much of their time in trees where it is safer.

Lifespan

In the wild, orangutans often live between thirty and forty years. They have been known to live past forty years in **captivity.**

Orangutans are adults by the time they are between twelve and fifteen years old.

Some adult male orangutans
have special cheek pads on their
faces. They are usually larger than
males that don't have them.

Population

All three kinds of orangutans are **endangered**. There are not many left in the wild.

Both the Sumatran and Tapanuli orangutans are **critically endangered**. They are very close to being **extinct** in the wild.

There are thought to be fewer than 70,000 Bornean orangutans, 7,500 Sumatran orangutans, and 900 Tapanuli orangutans left in the wild.

Orangutans in Danger

The biggest threat that orangutans are facing is habitat loss. Their rainforests homes are being cut down for the wood and building.

In the past, orangutans have been caught by humans to be kept as pets or in zoos.

Helping Orangutans

Many people are trying to help orangutans. There are special **conservancies** where orangutans that are sick or injured are taken care of.

They also provide orangutans with a habitat where they will be safe.

There are laws in place that protect orangutans from being caught and removed from their habitat.

People are also trying to learn more about orangutans. They hope that learning more about them will allow us to help them more.

Glossary

Captivity: animals that are kept by humans, not in the wild

Climate: the weather in a particular place

Conservancy: an organization that works to protect animals or natural resources

Critically Endangered: very close to becoming extinct

Diurnal: active during the day

Endangered: at risk of becoming

extinct

Extinct: no more left in the wild

Mimic: to copy

Omnivore: an animal that eats

meat and plants

Predator: an animal that hunts other

animals

Solitary: living alone

Territorial: when an animal will fight

to protect the land it claims as its

own

About the Author

Victoria Blakemore is a first grade

teacher in Southwest Florida with a

passion for reading.

You can visit her at

www.elementaryexplorers.com

Also in This Series

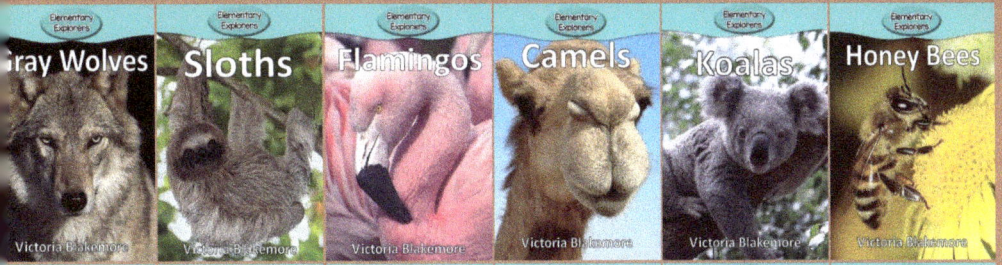

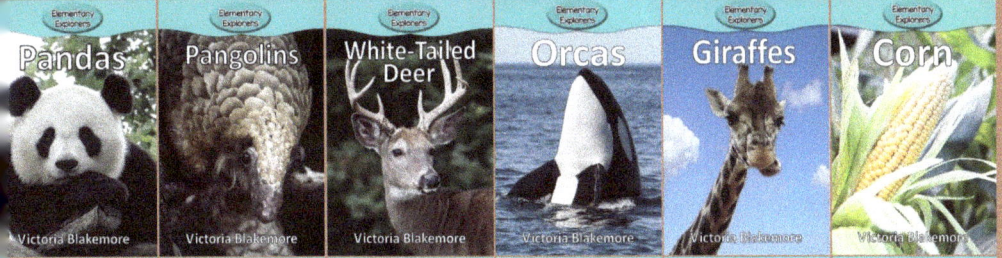

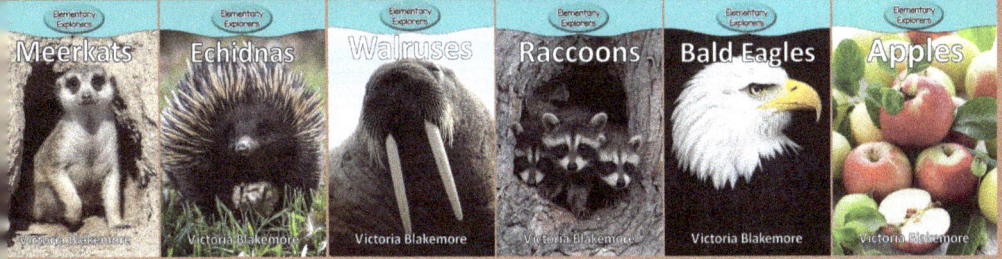

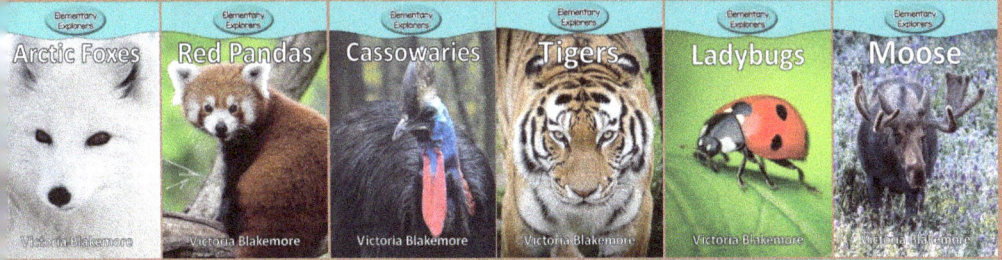

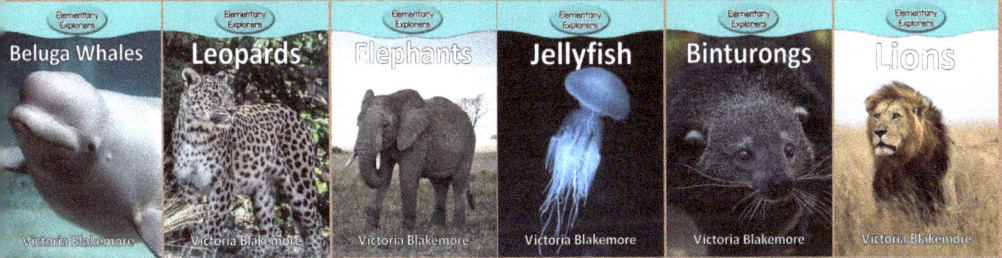

Gray Wolves — Victoria Blakemore
Sloths — Victoria Blakemore
Flamingos — Victoria Blakemore
Camels — Victoria Blakemore
Koalas — Victoria Blakemore
Honey Bees — Victoria Blakemore

Pandas — Victoria Blakemore
Pangolins — Victoria Blakemore
White-Tailed Deer — Victoria Blakemore
Orcas — Victoria Blakemore
Giraffes — Victoria Blakemore
Corn — Victoria Blakemore

Meerkats — Victoria Blakemore
Echidnas — Victoria Blakemore
Walruses — Victoria Blakemore
Raccoons — Victoria Blakemore
Bald Eagles — Victoria Blakemore
Apples — Victoria Blakemore

Arctic Foxes — Victoria Blakemore
Red Pandas — Victoria Blakemore
Cassowaries — Victoria Blakemore
Tigers — Victoria Blakemore
Ladybugs — Victoria Blakemore
Moose — Victoria Blakemore

Beluga Whales — Victoria Blakemore
Leopards — Victoria Blakemore
Elephants — Victoria Blakemore
Jellyfish — Victoria Blakemore
Binturongs — Victoria Blakemore
Lions — Victoria Blakemore

Dolphins — Victoria Blakemore
Reindeer — Victoria Blakemore
Hammerhead Sharks — Victoria Blakemore
Hippos — Victoria Blakemore
Pumpkins — Victoria Blakemore
Peafowl — Victoria Blakemore

Also in This Series

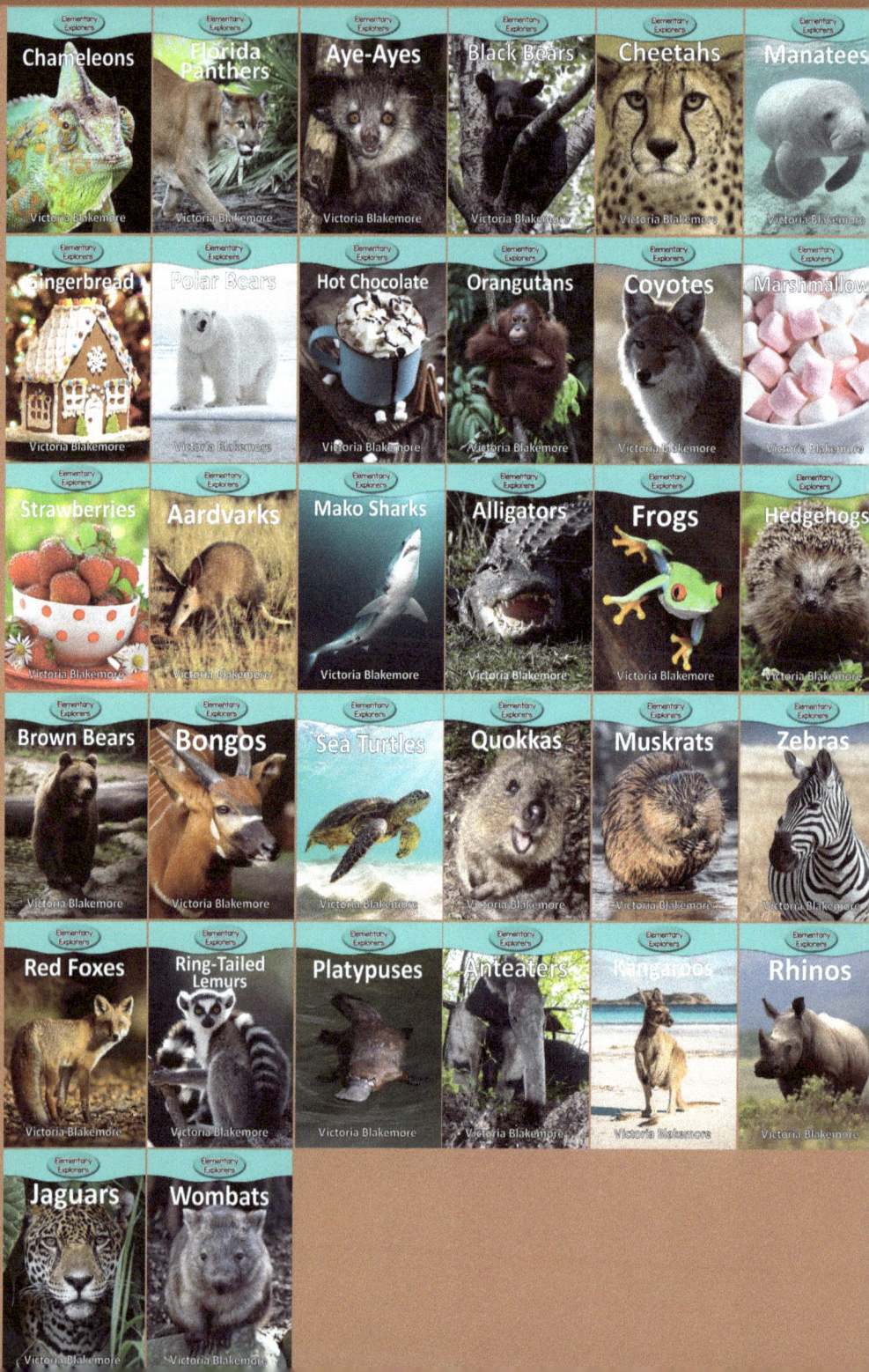

Chameleons — Victoria Blakemore
Florida Panthers — Victoria Blakemore
Aye-Ayes — Victoria Blakemore
Black Bears — Victoria Blakemore
Cheetahs — Victoria Blakemore
Manatees — Victoria Blakemore

Gingerbread — Victoria Blakemore
Polar Bears — Victoria Blakemore
Hot Chocolate — Victoria Blakemore
Orangutans — Victoria Blakemore
Coyotes — Victoria Blakemore
Marshmallow — Victoria Blakemore

Strawberries — Victoria Blakemore
Aardvarks — Victoria Blakemore
Mako Sharks — Victoria Blakemore
Alligators — Victoria Blakemore
Frogs — Victoria Blakemore
Hedgehogs — Victoria Blakemore

Brown Bears — Victoria Blakemore
Bongos — Victoria Blakemore
Sea Turtles — Victoria Blakemore
Quokkas — Victoria Blakemore
Muskrats — Victoria Blakemore
Zebras — Victoria Blakemore

Red Foxes — Victoria Blakemore
Ring-Tailed Lemurs — Victoria Blakemore
Platypuses — Victoria Blakemore
Anteaters — Victoria Blakemore
Kangaroos — Victoria Blakemore
Rhinos — Victoria Blakemore

Jaguars — Victoria Blakemore
Wombats — Victoria Blakemore